All About Sharks

Carmel Reilly

Contents

What Are Sharks?	2
What Sharks Look Like	4
What Sharks Eat	8
Types of Sharks	10
Amazing Sharks	16
Why Sharks Need To Be Protected	17
Glossary	23
Index	24

What Are Sharks?

Sharks are a type of fish.
They are one of the oldest animals on our planet.
They have lived on Earth since before the time of the dinosaurs.

Sharks can be found in oceans all around the world, except for cold areas around the Arctic and Antarctic. Some sharks live near the surface of the water, while others live deep in the ocean.

There are more than 400 **species** of shark.

What Sharks Look Like

Most sharks have long, narrow bodies,
with dark-colored backs and light-colored underbellies.
They are covered with very thick skin,
which is made up of thousands of small, rough scales.

Sharks breathe through their gills.
Each shark has between five and seven gills
on each side of its head.

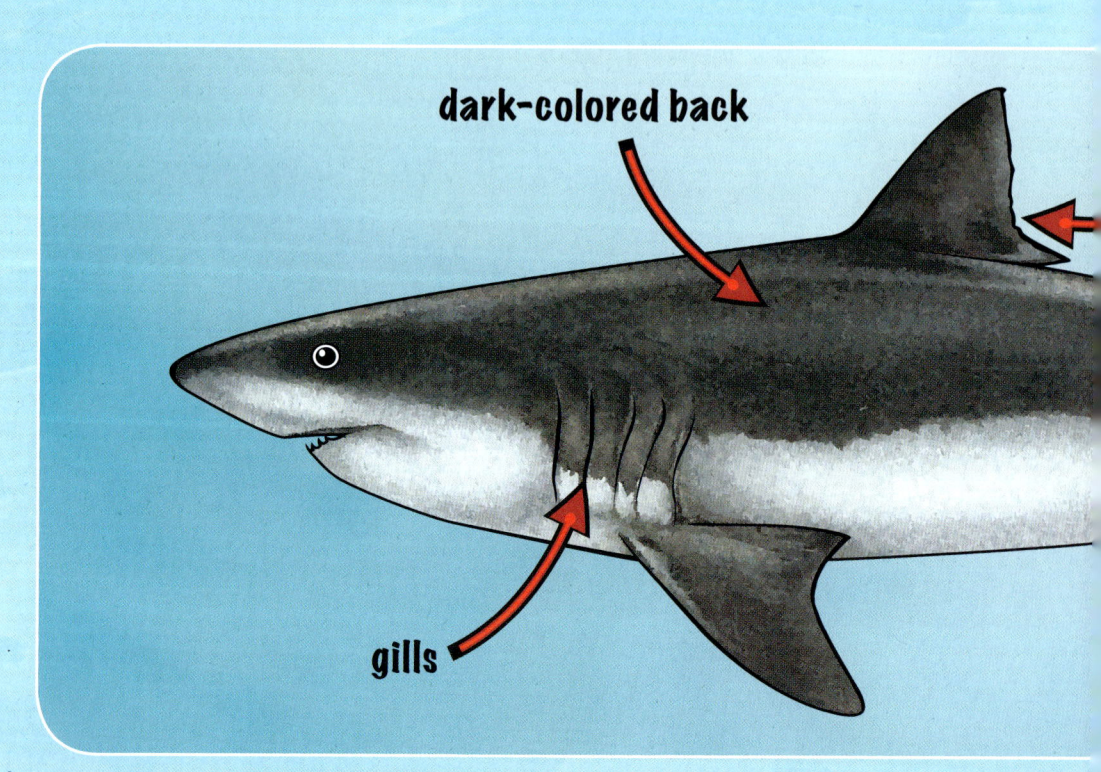

dark-colored back

gills

Sharks have eight fins and a strong tail, which help to steer and **propel** them through the water.

The smallest sharks are less than eight inches long.
The largest sharks can be more than 40 feet in length.

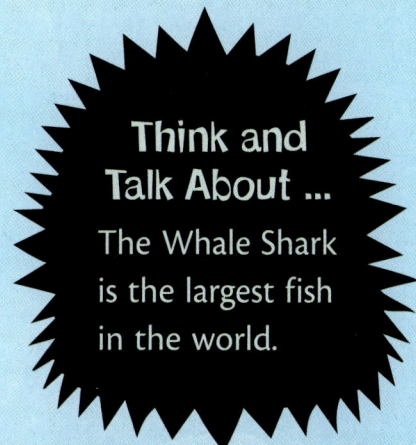

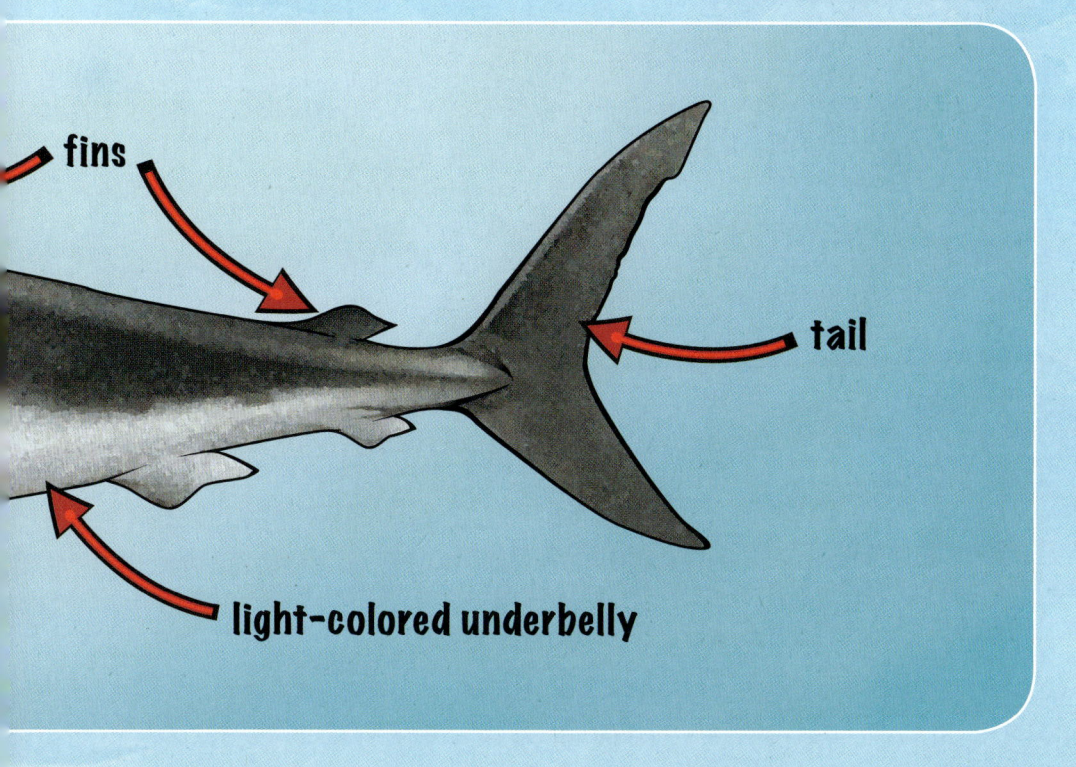

Think and Talk About ...
The Whale Shark is the largest fish in the world.

fins

tail

light-colored underbelly

Sharks' Skeletons

Sharks do not have bones like other fish. Instead, their skeletons are made of cartilage. Cartilage is not as heavy as bone. It can bend more easily, helping sharks to move quickly through the water.

Think and Talk About ...
The ears and noses of humans are made of cartilage.

A Blacktail Reef Shark uses its bendable cartilage skeleton to swim.

Sharks' Teeth

Sharks have two or three rows of sharp teeth for tearing food.
They often lose their teeth, but when this happens,
new teeth grow in their place.
Sharks can grow thousands of new teeth during their lives.

Sharks use their sharp teeth when hunting for food.

What Sharks Eat

Most sharks are **predators**,
which means they hunt for their food.
Larger sharks eat all types of fish.
They also hunt for and eat bigger sea animals,
such as small whales, seals, and even other sharks.
Sharks that live near the bottom of the ocean
usually eat a lot of shellfish and crabs.

A Lemon Shark swims over seagrass.

A Whale Shark can open its mouth to more than three feet wide.

There are a few species of shark that do not hunt. Instead, they **filter** tiny sea creatures through their mouths and gills.

Types of Sharks

Spiny Dogfish Sharks

Spiny Dogfish Sharks are the most common of all sharks. They are unusual, because they have two poisonous spikes, called spines, near their back fins.
These spines protect them from attackers.

Spiny Dogfish Sharks usually live in cool waters not far from the shore.
They eat many types of fish, including smaller sharks.

Think and Talk About ...
Some Spiny Dogfish Sharks can live up to 100 years.

spine

spine

Dwarf Lantern Sharks

Dwarf Lantern Sharks are the smallest of all sharks. They only grow to about seven inches long. These sharks live in warm waters near Central America.

Think and Talk About ...
Dwarf Lantern Sharks glow brightly in the dark, like lanterns.

Hammerhead Sharks

Hammerhead Sharks have large, wide heads. They have eyes on either side of their heads to help them to see things
in different directions at the same time.

During the day, Hammerhead Sharks swim in large schools, or groups.
Hammerhead Sharks hunt all kinds of fish, but stingrays are their favorite food.

These sharks are called "Hammerheads" because their heads look like hammers.

Wobbegong Sharks

Wobbegong Sharks live in the ocean
near Australia and Indonesia.
They spend most of their time on the seabed in shallow waters.
These sharks have patterns on their backs, which help them
to blend into the sand.

This Wobbegong Shark is using its patterned back to hide on the ocean floor.

Great White Sharks

Great White Sharks are large sharks that can grow up to 20 feet long.

They hunt and eat seals and seabirds, as well as fish. When they have eaten a large meal, they do not have to eat again for as long as 2 months.

Think and Talk About ... Great White Sharks can have as many as 3,000 teeth.

Great White Sharks are at the top of the food chain.

Whale Sharks

Whale Sharks are the largest species of shark. They can grow to almost 40 feet in length.

Whale Sharks eat by filtering tiny sea creatures and small fish through their mouths. They swim thousands of miles every year in search of food.

Whale Sharks are the biggest sharks in the world.

Amazing Sharks

The ocean needs predators such as sharks.
Predators keep the numbers of fish in the ocean in balance.
They also help to keep groups of fish and their **habitats** healthy.

Sharks are amazing creatures.
They have been on our planet for millions of years.
They are an important part of our oceans.

Why Sharks Need To Be Protected

Every year, more than 100 million sharks are killed by people fishing with huge nets from boats in the ocean.
Shark **populations** are becoming smaller.
Soon, there will not be enough sharks to keep the ocean healthy.
Sharks need to be protected so that their numbers can increase again.

Sharks Control the Number of Fish in the Ocean

Every living thing in the sea depends on another living thing for food. Plants and tiny sea creatures are eaten by fish. Fish are then eaten by larger fish, or predators.

large sharks (top predators)

large fish and other sea creatures

A lot of sharks are top predators.
Top predators eat many types of fish,
but no other fish eat them.

Top predators are important, because
they keep fish populations from growing too large.
They control the number of fish in the ocean
and keep different fish groups balanced.

small fish

plants and tiny sea creatures

Sharks Keep Fish Populations Healthy

Sharks eat fish that are weak or unwell. This helps to keep fish populations healthy and free from diseases.

Sharks Help To Protect Ocean Habitats

As well as eating fish, sharks also scare fish away from some areas.
In seagrass beds, sharks scare away sea animals, such as stingrays.
Stingrays can eat and destroy seagrass beds.
Seagrass beds do not just provide food for many fish,
they are also places where fish live and breed.
If seagrass is destroyed, whole populations of fish will die out.

What If Sharks Die Out?

Some people think that if sharks die out, there will be more fish in the ocean. But scientists believe that if sharks die out, many other types of fish will also die. Some fish populations will get diseases. Other fish populations will grow too large and eat and destroy other fish and plants.

Sharks need to be protected to make sure that all ocean life stays safe and healthy.

Glossary

filter *(verb)* — to separate solids (such as tiny sea creatures) from liquids by passing the liquid through small gaps (such as a shark's gills)

habitats *(noun)* — the places where plants or animals naturally exist

populations *(noun)* — groups of a type of plant or animal

predators *(noun)* — animals that hunt and kill other animals for food

propel *(verb)* — to cause something to move forwards

species *(noun)* — different types of the same family of plant or animal

Index

Blacktail Reef Shark   6
cartilage   6
crabs   8
diseases   20, 22
Dwarf Lantern Shark   11
fins   5, 10
fish   2, 5–6, 8, 10, 12, 14–16, 18–22
fishing   17
food   7–8, 12, 15, 18, 21, 23
gills   4, 9, 23
Great White Shark   14
habitats   16, 21, 23
Hammerhead Shark   12
Lemon Shark   8
ocean   3, 8, 13, 16–19, 21–22

plant   18, 22–23
populations   17, 19–23
predators   8, 16, 18–19, 23
scales   4
seabirds   14
seagrass   8, 21
seals   8, 14
shellfish   8
species   3, 9, 23
Spiny Dogfish Shark   10
stingrays   12, 21
teeth   7, 14
whales   8
Whale Shark   5, 9, 15
Wobbegong Shark   13